# TRIUMPH
# T90 & T100
# UNIT TWINS

1960 - 1974

**Roy Bacon**

First published in the United Kingdom by:
Niton Publishing
PO Box 3. Ventnor. Isle of Wight PO38 2AS

Acknowledgements
The author would like to thank those who
helped this book by supplying the photo-
graphs. Most came from the EMAP archives
or *Motor Cycle News* by courtesy of the
editor Peter Bolt. Others came from the
Mick Woollet archive and some from the
author's files. That of the T100SC came
from owner Phil Taylor, and three were taken
by professional Cecil Bailey.

This edition published 1995 by
The Promotional Reprint Company Ltd.
exclusively for Selecta Book Limited.
Roundway. Devizes. Wiltshire SN10 2HR
and Reed Editions in Australia.

ISBN 1 85648 308 8

Printed in Hong Kong

Export T100C of 1970 with its lovely twin, waist-level exhaust systems.

# Contents

# Introduction

'Tiger 90' was a model name first used by Edward Turner for a pre-war sports single. It was the largest of a trio of Tiger models he introduced to brighten up the rather staid Triumph range and, while the changes were mainly restricted to chrome-plating and polish rather than serious engine tuning, the result was most successful.

The 250, 350 and 500 cc Tigers had numbers attached to their names to suggest their top speeds of 70, 80 and 90 mph respectively. With the introduction of the 500 cc Speed Twin for 1938, it was inevitable that this would be followed by a sports version, so the twin-cylinder Tiger 100 replaced the Tiger 90 single for 1939.

After the war, the Tiger 100 continued as the sports 500 up to 1959, during which time it was joined by the larger Tiger 110 and Bonneville models. In 1957 the first of the small unit twins appeared as the 349 cc Twenty One, or 3TA. Two years later, this was joined by the 5TA, which replaced the original Speed Twin, but kept its name.

For 1960 the pre-unit T100 design was replaced by the unit-construction T100A, which was based on the 5TA, even to the extent of including its touring rear enclosure. Its sober style was short-lived, however, for it became the stylish T100SS for 1962. This featured a rear skirt to enhance its lines. The next year brought a revival of the Tiger 90, but as a sports version of the 3TA.

In time, both models lost their skirts and, while the T90 ran on to 1969, the T100 was expanded into a range of models from 1966. Among them was the twin-carburettor Daytona, which brought the Tiger back to its original sporting roots and in this way the sports twins ran to 1974 and their finish. Right at the end came a small, pre-production batch of Series 2 machines with the later BSA/Triumph Group forks and hubs.

The machine is a 1962 T100SS with its skirts and style, while the picture is most likely of a bridge over the M45 near Meriden.

# The T100A

When the unit-construction T100A was launched there was little, other than finish and badges, to distinguish it from the touring Speed Twin and smaller Twenty-One. All three models featured the bathtub rear enclosure, nacelle forks and well-valanced front mudguard, while the bulk of the engine and gearbox unit was common.

Virtually all the cycle parts were common to all models, the main exception being the electrics. This was because the T100A featured energy-transfer (ET) ignition, which involved changes to switches, wiring, alternator and distributor. However, that excepted, only the colour varied from one model to another.

The engine unit came from the 349 cc Twenty-One, launched in 1957, and was enlarged to 490 cc by increasing

First of the small sports unit twin line was this 1960 T100A, despite its touring lines with full bathtub and well-valanced front mudguard.

For 1961 the T100A was lightened in appearance, having a silver paint finish for the bathtub and mudguard as well as the lower tank.

the bore from 58.25 to 69 mm, while retaining the 65.5 mm stroke. For the T100A, the compression ratio was raised from the 7.0:1 of the Speed Twin to 9.0:1, and there were revised camshafts as well as the ignition system change.

The crankcase was formed from two aluminium castings with the joint on the vertical centre-line of the engine, but then stepped over to the left so that the whole of the gearbox shell was included in the right-hand casting. The left-hand casting comprised the crankcase half and the primary chaincase inner

with an access door to the final drive sprocket. This door was a circular plate which carried an oil seal to run on the gearbox mainshaft. The right-hand casting included the crankcase half, which also formed the timing chest inner. The gearbox shell was formed behind the crankcase with a mounting lug at the top. The shell was open on the right to allow assembly of the shafts and gears. Each crankcase half had a filler cap in its top face, behind the cylinder block, one for the gearbox and the other for the primary chaincase. An oil filter went into the sump of the

Ginny and Bill Dorresteyn out on their TR5AR machines in 1961. These have road, rather than trail, fitments.

right-hand case half, and the oil pipes were connected to the rear of this area.

A ball race supported the left-hand end of the crankshaft, with an oil seal outboard of it, while the right-hand end was looked after by a flanged bush. The crankshaft itself was a one-piece forging to which the central flywheel was retained by three radial bolts. A sludge trap was built into the crankpins, and oil for the big-ends entered the shaft via the flanged bush and various drillings.

Light-alloy connecting-rods with shell big-end bearings and bushed little-ends were used. The three-ring pistons were held by hollow gudgeon pins retained by circlips,

and they were formed to give the higher compression ratio. They moved in a cast-iron, silver finished, block, the whole of the engine top half being of typical Triumph construction.

Thus, the block had a tappet housing pressed into its base flange fore and aft on the engine centre-line, each being retained by a single set screw. The block itself sat on a gasket and was held down by nuts on eight short studs, while the light-alloy cylinder head was held to it by eight bolts with a gasket between the two parts.

The cylinder head was from the Speed Twin with all detail parts common. It had adaptors screwed into each exhaust port for the pipes

A 1961 T100A out on test, showing the engine lines that were to remain common to the type throughout production.

to clamp to, and there was a manifold on the inlet side. This carried an Amal Monobloc type 375 carburettor of 7/8 in. bore which was connected to an air filter by a short rubber hose. The valve guides were pressed

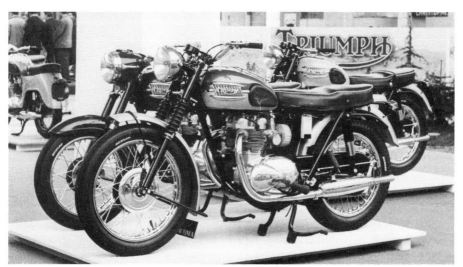

A 1961 TR5AR on show in France that year. This model was neither shown nor even reported on in its home country.

The T100SS replaced the T100A for 1962 and had a much more sporting line with its skirt and separate headlamp shell. This was the only year for the distributor ignition system.

into a circlip location, and each had a cup fitted round it for the duplex springs to seat on. A collar and collets retained each set of springs and their valve, there being separate valve wells for the inlets and exhausts.

An aluminium rocker box sat over each well and incorporated a single spindle on which were fitted two rockers and an array of hardened and spring washers to deal with wear and end-float. An O-ring went at one end as a seal; oil was supplied to the other from the main return line. Each rocker had a ball pin fitted to its inner arm, and an adjuster and locknut to its outer arm. Access to these for setting the valve gaps was

via four large threaded caps with crossed slots for turning them. Pushrods connected the tappets in their housings to the rockers, and these were enclosed by chrome-plated tubes with seals at each end.

The tappets were raised by camshafts which ran across the engine, high up in the crankcase, to fore and aft of the crankshaft. They were driven by gear from the crankshaft, a pinion mounted on the right-hand end being meshed with an intermediate gear which drove both camshaft gears. There were bushes to support the left-hand shaft ends, but the right-hand ends were larger and ran directly in the crankcase. Each camshaft was held

That 1962 T100SS moved on from the motorway bridge to well into the Welsh hills, Abbey Cwmhir being a very small hamlet indeed.

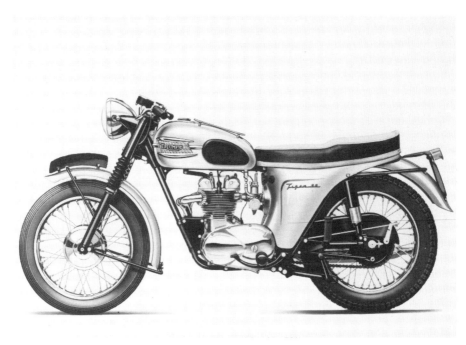

The Tiger 90 was introduced for 1963 with the skirt and siamesed pipes of the larger sports twin, but it had the points in the timing cover from the start.

in place by a plate fitted in the timing chest. The inlet camshaft, at the rear, also had three other functions to drive.

From its left-hand end, the inlet camshaft drove a timed, disc-valve breather which was matched to a fixed disc fitted in behind the camshaft bush. A breather pipe was pressed into the underside of the crankcase and had a rubber extension. The nut on the right-hand camshaft end was formed with an offset pin which drove the twin-plunger oil pump of the dry-sump lubrication system. This pump was bolted to a face beneath the inlet camshaft in the timing chest and

was a typical Triumph type, having a drive block to move the plungers. The scavenge pump was larger than the feed, while both had ball valves to control the oil flow.

The third function driven by the inlet camshaft was the ignition distributor. This assembly, complete with contact points and auto-advance, went behind the right-hand side of the block, its shaft being driven by a skew gear cut on the camshaft. A separate coil was used and its high-tension current was distributed by a rotor under the cap. A rubber sheath enclosed the cap and the three high-tension cables to give a tidy line to this area.

To suit the energy-transfer ignition, the distributor had a special cam, the ignition coil was a Lucas type 2ET, and the alternator an RM15 with the rotor pegged to the engine sprocket. This timed it to the crankshaft for a maximum-energy pulse when the points opened, but the timing overall was quite critical and not helped by the backlash in the distributor skew-gear drive.

The timing chest was enclosed by a cover of triangular shape which carried the Triumph patent plate. A pressure release valve and indicator button went into the front of the timing chest, on the line of the crankshaft, to regulate the system pressure and assure the rider that it was functioning as required.

The alternator was mounted on the left-hand side of the engine in the primary chaincase, outboard of the duplex primary chain. The chain ran back to a conventional clutch and its tension was set by a slipper blade under the lower run, this being adjusted from the rear. The access plug for this was in the cast-alloy chaincase outer, which was retained by a row of screws round its edge and had a single large plug for replenishing the oil.

The clutch was typically

The T100SS also had the timing-cover points for 1963, but otherwise stayed as introduced.

Triumph, a hub being mounted on the gearbox mainshaft with a key and taper. The hub formed the inner race of the drum roller bearing and was splined for the clutch centre. The centre incorporated a transmission shock absorber, with four shock and rebound rubbers, and was splined on its outer diameter for the six plain driven plates. The five drive plates, with bonded-on friction material, were splined to the drum, and the whole assembly was clamped up by the pressure plate and four springs. An adjuster went in the centre of the pressure plate, as the quick-thread

lift mechanism, on the right-hand side of the machine, did not have this feature and simply transmitted its movement to the clutch via a ball-bearing and the pushrod.

A conventional British design of gearbox was housed in the right-hand crankcase casting, with inner and outer covers to enclose the mechanism. The layshaft was positioned aft of the mainshaft, which ran through the sleeve gear carrying the final-drive sprocket on the left. Two ball races and several bushes supported the shafts, while two selectors, controlled by a single quadrant-shaped camplate above

A 1963 Tiger 90 out on test that year, showing its sporting lines and Triumph pedigree well.

Both the skirt and the siamesed pipes were dropped from the Tiger 90 for 1964.

the shafts, selected the gears. The design allowed the gearbox to be built up in the inner cover which was then assembled to the shell.

The positive-stop mechanism was simple and went between the two covers, the pedal being positioned on the right. As usual for Triumph, the movement was 'down-for-down', and the selected gear was shown by a small pointer and scale fitted to the top of the inner cover. The folding kickstart also went on the right, there being a pawl and ratchet mechanism within the layshaft first gear, and a clock spring to return the lever.

A two-part frame housed the engine and gearbox unit, with small mounting plates at the rear, larger ones at the front and stays to the rocker boxes. The front section of the frame had single top, down and seat tubes with duplex rails beneath the power unit. The top tube was lower than usual, so it was turned up at its forward end to join the forged headstock. This somewhat weak layout was stiffened by a beam member that was incorporated into the petrol tank. This tank was bolted into place and, while the beam ran right through it, some frame stress must have been transmitted to the tank and its welded joints.

The rear frame section comprised a loop that ran round the seat, twin tubes running down from

The 1964 T100SS copied the T90 in the cosmetic changes, and both were fitted with a switch panel on the left to match the oil tank.

the rear-unit upper mountings to the ends of the under-engine rails, and various braces and brackets. Bolted-on supports carried the pillion rests and supported the low-level silencers which, for the T100A, had mutes fitted as standard, these being an option for the other unit models. The exhaust pipes were held to the port stubs by finned clamps and further supported by small brackets attached to either end of one of the front engine mounting studs.

The seat tube incorporated a lug for the rear pivoted-fork spindle, which was pressed into place. As the fork bushes turned on the spindle ends, the spindle had to be removed if the bushes needed

replacement, which was not at all easy.

The whole frame design showed that it had been laid down for a touring 350. The rear fork was controlled by Girling spring-and-damper units fitted with stock springs, but both harder and softer ones were available. Both centre and prop stands were provided, the footrests were bolted to the frame with some adjustment, and the brake pedal went on the left with a rod running straight back to the cam lever. Front suspension was by stock Triumph telescopic forks with hydraulic damping, and these turned in cup-and-cone head races. A steering damper was fitted beneath the lower crown and set by a knob above the top one, while the upper area of the forks was enclosed by the Triumph nacelle.

The nacelle, first introduced for 1949, was in three sections: two lower pieces, which included the upper fork stanchion shrouds, and the top. The assembly carried the headlight unit, with a horn grille beneath it, and the top was used to mount the speedometer, ammeter, light switch and cut-out button. Thanks to the energy-transfer ignition, the switches, and thus the top, differed from that fitted to the touring models.

A full-width hub was used in the front wheel and was of composite construction, steel pressings being brazed together and riveted into the cast-iron brake drum. The hub turned on ball races, and its one-piece spindle was held in the forks by caps. The drum housed a 7 in. single-leading-shoe brake, and the hub was laced to a steel rim with straight spokes, the tyre size being 3.25 x 17 in.

At the rear, there was another 7 in. single-leading-shoe brake and a 17 in. rim, but the tyre section was 3.50 in., the spokes angled and the

Drive-side of the 1965 Tiger 90, which had changed little from the previous year, although a frame brace went up under the tank.

drum offset. A quickly-detachable wheel was listed as an option, but both wheels were similar, having a sprocket that was integral with the drum, provision to drive the speedometer, and a hub with small spoke flanges.

The style of the unit-construction twins was set by their rear enclosure, which ran from the carburettor to the rear number plate and down from the seat. The sides were not completely filled in, so much of the wheel was visible. The result had the lines of an inverted hip-bath, which quickly led to the 'bathtub

Triumph' name.

The T100A copied the tourers and was fitted with the same enclosure, there being just a change of motif on the side. An inner rear mudguard went under the bathtub to keep road dirt and rainwater under some control, while the model was fitted with the same well-valanced front mudguard as the other machines. This was supported by a centre bridge and a rear stay which doubled as a front stand. The front number plate had the stock Triumph surround, dating from 1939, which gave it style and line,

The 1965 T100SS was, again, as the T90, with frame brace added and little other change.

The export T100SC of 1965, this fine example being shown in 1990 after a full rebuild.

but in this case needed a packing piece to make it fit the mudguard curvature correctly.

The dualseat matched the top of the bathtub and was hinged along one side with a catch to hold it down. Under it went a moulded rubber toolpad, into which the toolkit items were fitted, and this sat on the inner rear mudguard. The oil tank went under the seat nose, on the right, with the battery beside it and the air filter in front of that.

The petrol tank carried the Triumph grille badges of the period, which were flanked by styling strips fore and aft. Kneegrips were fitted, as was the useful parcel grid, and the tank had a bayonet filler cap,

single petrol tap with filter and reserve, and a central styling strip running from front to rear.

Stock handlebars and controls, as used by the tourers, were fitted, and the combined horn button and dip switch was mounted on the back of the clutch lever. American handlebars were available, as an option, with longer control cables to suit.

Finish for the T100A was predominantly black, but this was relieved by ivory for the lower petrol tank. A gold line marked the join, where not concealed by the styling strips, and the wheel rims and other details were chrome-plated.

# Sports styling appears

The performance of the T100A was improved for 1961 by a change of camshaft and an increase in carburettor size to a 1 in. type 376 Monobloc. The gearing was lowered by one tooth on the gearbox sprocket, and braking was improved by a change to floating brake shoes for both wheels. The moulded toolpad was replaced by a prosaic roll, and the finish was brightened by using silver for the lower tank, front mudguard and bathtub. During the year, the awkward energy-transfer ignition was dropped and the conventional coil ignition of the tourers adopted, along with their electrical details and switches.

The T100A was joined by three variants of the off-road, or

For 1966 there was a new tank badge for this Tiger 90 and the other models.

competition, TR5A model for 1961, the specification of these depending on their market. All lacked the bathtub and well valanced front mudguard, and could have trail tyres, siamesed exhaust system and high bars with ball-ended levers. All were powered by the T100A engine unit and were based on the same cycle parts.

Despite the brighter 1961 finish, the T100A remained a sober model for the sports market and far too close to the tourers in appearance. Therefore, it was transformed into the T100SS for 1962. This had the lithe sporting lines associated with and expected of the Tiger models.

The engine unit and most of the cycle parts remained as before, but the alternator became a type RM19, there was a siamesed exhaust system leading to a single silencer low on the right, and a further lowering of the gearing. The bathtub was replaced by a much smaller skirt, which filled in the sub-frame corner, but left the wheel exposed. To go with this abbreviation, a standard rear mudguard was fitted and was matched at the front by a sports guard.

The 1966 T100, which had the plain dualseat top common to the twins that year and a revised frame with the top brace welded in.

Export T100C for 1966 with raised and siamesed exhaust system, plus other off-road features.

The front end was further amended by fitting gaiters to the forks, deleting the nacelle and replacing it with a separate, chrome-plated, headlamp shell. This only carried the ammeter, as a combined lights and ignition switch was mounted in the left-hand side skirt, while the speedometer was moved to the fork crown. The wheel hubs continued as they were, but the tyre sizes were changed to 3.25 x 19 in. at the front and 3.50 x 18 in. rear.

The finish for the T100SS reflected its style and line, Kingfisher blue being used for the tank top, mudguard stripes and rear skirt. This was matched by silver for the lower tank and both mudguards.

There was gold lining, while the other painted details were in black. The result, with the added chrome-plating, was a striking machine.

While two of the TR5A models continued for 1962, the third became the T100SC, a competition model with an off-road capability for the USA market. It retained the energy-transfer ignition system of the T100A and had lowered gearing, a smaller petrol tank and off-road tyres. With the smaller tank came a separate frame strut which was bolted in place to stiffen the frame, while the tank was held down by a strap. The model's finish was similar to that of the T100SS, but with burgundy in place of the Kingfisher blue.

The most obvious change for 1963 was the repositioning of the points into the timing cover, where their cam was driven from the exhaust camshaft via an auto-advance. The distributor was dispensed with, so there were two sets of points and twin coils, these being mounted above the engine. The change introduced a new exhaust camshaft which also drove the rev-counter gearbox from its left-hand end. A three-spring clutch replaced the earlier type, and the gearbox camplate was strengthened.

Externally, the skirt was given extra styling to enhance its looks and its ends were extended round the dualseat base. Separate switches were fitted in the left skirt for lights and ignition. The fuel tank was revised to provide space for the ignition coils, and the T100SS had its gearing lowered and an 18 in. front wheel fitted.

The T100SC continued, with its siamesed exhaust moved to waist-level on the left, and was joined by two new models. One was the export T100SR for the USA market. This was as the T100SS except for the high bars and a 19 in. front wheel. For the West Coast, it had a small 2 gallon tank, as used by the T100SC, but elsewhere it kept the standard 3 gallon one.

The second new model was the

Road-going Tiger 100 for 1966, out on test with one of the magazines.

New for 1967 was the twin-carburettor Daytona T100T model, named after the American race which the firm had won.

Tiger 90, effectively the T100SS fitted with the smaller, 349 cc engine. This reduced capacity came from a 58.25 mm bore, but the stroke remained at 65.5 mm and the compression ratio was 9.0:1. A 15/16 in. Monobloc supplied the mixture, and the gearing was lowered, but the

Timing-side of a 1967 Tiger 90, which had changed little from its introduction, although there was a new frame that year.

rest of the machine was common.

The finish was in Alaskan white for the petrol tank, mudguards and skirt with a gold stripe for each mudguard. The other painted parts were in black, and there was chrome-plating for the headlamp shell and wheel rims. The finish for the T100 models continued to be two-tone, as before, but in Regal purple for the tank top, mudguard stripes and skirt. The mudguards and lower tank stayed in silver.

The line of models was unaltered for 1964, but all lost their rear skirt.

In its place, there was a left-hand side panel which carried the two switches.

On the inside, the clutch mechanism was changed to a three-ball-and-ramp system, while the gearbox bushes completed their gradual change over to needle races. On the outside, the exhaust system was more of a touring type, a separate pipe being connected to a low-level silencer on each side for the SS, SR and T90 models. All had changes to the front forks, external springs being adopted, while

A Daytona Triumph T100T out on test in 1967. It was a very fast 500 for that time and popular with motorcyclists.

Engine unit and the twin Monobloc carburettors splayed out from the cylinder head of the 1967 T100T.

magnetic instrument heads replaced the older chronometric type. Only the SR model had a rev-counter fitted as standard, but this was an option for the SS and T90. The tyre sizes of the USA models were altered to 3.50 x 19 in. front for the SC, and 4.00 x 18 in. rear for the SR.

The T100 models kept to their earlier style of finish for 1964, but in scarlet and silver, the scarlet being applied to the upper portions of all tanks and used for the mudguard stripes of the SS and SR models. The SC had polished light-alloy mudguards to match its competition nature, while the T90 had its upper tank in gold, but otherwise was as

before. All models had the new side panel finished in black to match the oil tank.

The frame strut became a standard fitment for 1965, so the standard tank had its fixings amended to suit, while its capacity was increased to $3\frac{1}{2}$ gallons. A minor amendment to the engine was a location slot in the flywheel to enable top-dead-centre to be found easily, while the oil pressure indicator button went, so removing a potential oil leak. The finish for all three T100 models was in Burnished gold for the upper tank and mudguard stripes, with Alaskan white for the lower tank and mudguards. The rest of the painted parts were in black, and only the West Coast SC had alloy mudguards. The T90's finish was to the same style, but in Pacific blue and silver.

The model line-up was amended for 1966 to become the T90 and T100 (much as before), the T100R, or road, model for the USA, and the East and West Coast versions of the T100C, or competition, model. All had modified frames, the strut being welded in place, a new 'eyebrow' tank badge, kneegrips which were stuck on rather than held by two screws, a separate bolt-on rear sprocket and an oil feed to the rear chain from the oil tank.

Energy-transfer ignition was used for the T100C models, which had a small headlight shell that carried both lights and dip switches. The model had a handlebar-mounted cut-out button and siamesed exhaust pipes leading to a waist-level silencer on the left. High bars and off-road tyres were fitted, but there was no left-hand side cover.

The petrol tank was new, there being a 2 gallon one for the USA models and a 3 gallon one for the others. All the road machines went over to a 12 volt electric system with zener diode control of the alternator output, which allowed the fitment of higher wattage headlamp

The single-carburettor version of the Tiger 100 continued as the T100S, as it had evolved from the earlier models.

John Giles on his 490 cc Triumph twin during the 1962 Welsh Three Days Trial, in which he dropped n[...]

while riding to the fast schedule.

The new dualseat with quilted top that was used for the 1967 twins of all capacities, this one being a T100T.

bulbs. The finish was much as before, but in Grenadier red and Alaskan white for the T90, and Sherbourne green and Alaskan white for the T100 models. The T100C versions differed only in having a green tank with a white stripe on the top. For that year alone, white handlebar grips were specified.

# The Daytona

For 1967, the sports twins settled into a range that was to remain for some time, the Tiger 90 being supported by four Tiger 100 twins (two for the USA and two for the home market). The basic models were the T90 and T100S, the latter being a continuation of the T100 of the previous year with a single carburettor.

Of far more interest to the enthusiast was the T100T, or Daytona, model, which had twin 1-1/16 in. Monobloc carburettors mounted on separate inlet tracts joined by a balance pipe, a raised compression ratio of 9.75:1 and a more sporting exhaust camshaft. The name came from the success the firm had enjoyed at the 1966 Daytona races and were to repeat at the 1967 event. For the USA this machine became the T100R, while the final model was the T100C. The

The timing-side of this 1967 T100C can be seen more clearly, as the exhaust system is out of the way.

latter was in the style of the previous T100SC.

The frame was revised once more to a more conventional form, the top tube being larger than the brace below it. The support for the rear fork pivot was improved and the petrol tank mountings revised to suit the frame changes. A steering lock was added to the fork top crown, and the handlebars were rubber-mounted. All models had black cushioned handlebar grips and a quilted top to the dualseat.

For the electrics, the road models had the light switch moved to the headlamp shell to join the ammeter, which was flanked by two warning lights. The ignition switch remained in the left-hand side panel, the T100C having a panel without a switch. This model kept to the energy-transfer ignition and small headlamp shell, as before, but with one warning light added. The exhaust system of the T100C became twin pipes and

Drive-side of the 1967 Tiger 90, still much as that of the first T100A seven years earlier.

The twin exhaust systems of this 1968 T100C dominate the drive-side to give the machine its off-road style.

silencers, both running along the left-hand side of the machine at waist level. The other models continued with the twin low-level systems.

The finish for the 1967 T100 models followed the established style, and all were similar in Pacific blue and Alaskan white. The Tiger 90 followed suit, but in Hi-fi scarlet in place of the blue.

All five models continued for 1968 with a number of common changes. A small cover appeared in the primary chaincase to allow the ignition timing to be checked, using a strobe, and the zener diode was given a finned heat-sink mounting positioned under the headlamp shell. This shell had a toggle switch

for the lights, while the ignition switch was moved to the left-hand fork shroud. There were new-style kneegrips.

The front forks had shuttle damping, and the steering damper continued to be fitted, except on the T100R. All engines went over to Concentric carburettors, a single 624 instrument being fitted to the T90, while all T100s had the 626. The T100R and T100T had two of the latter. These two sports models had their front brake size increased to 8 in., but kept to the single-leading-shoe type. The hub design was altered to include a spoke flange on the brake side, which increased the brake-shoe width, but precluded the use of straight spokes on that side.

The T100C alone had its ignition system changed to a capacitor type powered by the alternator. The finishes for 1968 kept to the existing style, except for the T100C, which had the petrol tank in a single colour and polished stainless-steel mudguards. The colour for all T100 models was Aquamarine green matched with silver, except on the T100C, while the T90 was in Riviera blue and silver.

There were a good number of alterations for 1969, the major one to the engine being an improvement to the main bearings. The drive-side bearing became a roller race, while the timing-side bush was replaced by a ball race. This required a revision to the lubrication system, an oil feed being directed into the end of the crankshaft - a much better arrangement.

An oil pressure switch went into the front edge of the timing cover, and an RM21 alternator replaced the earlier type. The exhaust pipes were joined by a balance pipe close to the ports, except on the T100C. The latter had a connector added between the pipes and silencers, this area being protected by a wire-mesh grille.

Timing-side of a 1968 T100S which offered good performance without the chore of keeping twin carburettors in synchronisation.

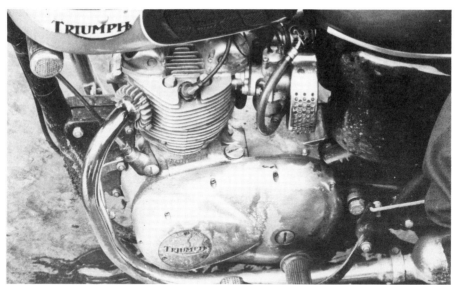

Engine unit of a 1968 Daytona with the rev-counter drive taken from the end of the exhaust camshaft and Concentric carburettors.

The front forks were spaced out a little further to enable a wider tyre to be fitted, and this meant that new fork crowns and a longer wheel spindle were required. The brake sizes remained as they were, but all

The Tiger 90 for 1968, when it continued with no real alterations and offered good performance for its capacity.

front brakes were changed to a twin-leading-shoe type. This had a die-cast backplate which incorporated the anchor lug, an air scoop (with gauze) and air exit slots. A bell-crank lever was used at the front cam so that the control cable could run neatly down the fork leg, and a rod joined the front and rear cam levers.

The model T100T had its front tyre size changed to 3.25 x 19 in., and all models had a new 'picture frame' tank badge. The parcel grid was no longer available, having been phased out on the USA models over the years, and a seat handrail appeared on the T100R and T100C.

The 1969 Tiger 100 finish was Lincoln green and silver, the T100C continuing with its single tank colour and stainless-steel mudguards.

Only the Tiger 100 models continued for 1970. They had a modified engine breathing system in which the timed disc valve was dispensed with, as was the drive-side oil seal, so that the engine breathed into the primary chaincase. The last was amended to include an outlet stub bolted to the back of the inner chaincase, above the gearbox sprocket. The hole in the case that led to this stub was masked by a plate inside the

A 1968 T100T. The left exhaust valve cap is missing, a common enough occurence with a Triumph twin.

The single-carburettor T100S for 1968, when it was fitted with the Concentric in place of the earlier Monobloc.

chaincase, allowing air to escape easily, but the oil tended to drain back.

The only chassis change was to make the steering damper an optional fitting. The finish colours became Jacaranda purple and silver, purple being the mudguard colour. The front mudguard alone had a silver stripe, although the T100C continued with stainless-steel mudguards. For that model the tank was in purple with a silver central stripe; the T100R had the purple with a silver waist; the T100T had the traditional purple upper and silver lower tank; but the T100S was in purple only.

# Final days

The model line-up was changed for 1971, with just the T100R and T100C continuing, but in USA, and UK and general-export versions. The latter continued as the T100T and T100S of the past, but with megaphone silencers not found on the USA-bound machines. The engine had access plugs added to the sides of the rocker boxes to facilitate setting the valve gaps, and the oil system was given a one-piece pressure release valve in place of the old type which could be dismantled.

The headlight mounting brackets were rubber-mounted to the fork shrouds, and the electrics were revised. The ammeter was dropped, but turn signals appeared, along with Lucas handlebar switches and buttons built into the control-lever pivot blocks. The operation of these was none too clear, but between

For 1969, the twin-leading-shoe front brake with bell-crank operation appeared on the 490 cc twins, this being the T100S.

The Daytona T100T of 1969 lost its rear suspension covers, but did keep the front fork gaiters.

them they covered horn, dip, indicators, headlamp flasher and kill switch.

Side reflectors were fitted to all models, having been used on machines for the USA since 1968, the front ones being under the tank nose in amber, while the rear ones were red. The rear reflectors had originally been mounted on the sides of the rear light support, but now were moved to the seat handrail so that the turn-signals could be mounted on the lamp support. At the front, the turn-signal supports were screwed into the sides of the headlamp shell and carried the lamps on their ends.

The quickly-detachable rear wheel was no longer listed. The finish colour was Olympic Flame with black for the mudguard stripes and a broad petrol tank waist band on the T100R. The T100C continued with its stainless mudguards, while its tank was in the Flame colour only.

Little was altered for 1972, other than the fixings of the exhaust pipes to the ports. The long-used stubs were dispensed with, the pipes becoming a push-fit in the cylinder head. However, the finned clamps were retained for decoration. The finish remained in the style of 1971, but with Cherry in place of the Flame.

For 1973, only the T100R was listed, still in two forms, as the T100C had been replaced by the TR5T

The 1969 twin-leading-shoe front brake with the bell-crank front cam lever, which allowed the cable to run straight up the fork leg.

Trophy Trail, or Adventurer, which used the same basic engine in a new frame. Changes to the Tiger were minor, but did include a return to the old type of oil pressure release valve.

The handlebar switch functions were changed a little, and the rear turn signals were moved to the reflector mounting on the seat

Drive-side of the 1969 T100S, which was still much as its predecessors, but had gained the strobe access cover in the chaincase from 1968.

handrail. The reflectors were incorporated in the sides of the rear lamp lens to allow this. The finish of the mudguards was changed to chrome-plating, and both the colour and style of the petrol tank finish were altered. The upper finish was run over the front shoulders of the tank and down to the top of the badge, the rest of the tank being in the second colour. For the USA, the upper colour was Ice white and the lower, Hi-fi vermilion, but for the UK and general-export machines, the colours were gold and Astral blue.

During the late 1960s the Triumph personnel had begun to feel the effects of control by their parent company, BSA. A design centre had been established at Umberslade Hall to serve both Meriden and Small Heath, while various aspects of running Triumph were transferred to BSA's control. This type of action had all the earmarks of a management disaster, with split responsibility and authority, plus ample opportunity for blame to be pushed to and fro.

The old Triumph hands longed

Daytona T100T timing-side, as for 1970 and little altered from the previous year.

for the days of Edward Turner, who had driven the firm along in a high-handed, dictatorial style, but one that had worked well and profitably. After his retirement, they had seen his tight organisation become slack and over-staffed from remote management.

This problem and its effects reached a climax late in 1970 when the group staged a lavish presentation of its new model range for both BSA and Triumph. This introduced new models, for which production drawings, much less tooling, were not available, and very major changes to the group's 650 cc twins. These had been restyled and given a new frame, forks and hubs

but, they were far from ready for the production line.

It was to be months before the big twins were ready to be built but, fortunately for Triumph, the Tiger 100 had not received any of the new group ministrations. This, at least, allowed the firm to build them, but only until they had consumed the normal annual production run of parts.

The factory finally went back to its 650s, while other proposed new models were never to reach production. All this cost a great deal of money, for the same problems, and worse, had arisen at the BSA plant. As a result, the group moved into deep financial trouble. This led

The 1970 T100S, which continued to offer a fine ride and good performance, coupled with reasonable fuel consumption.

The 1971 Daytona T100R escaped most of the group changes, so it retained the older type of forks and hubs. This is a USA model with tubular silencers.

to much activity in the composition of the main board and its relationship with all the group companies.

Finances went from bad to worse in 1972, and by the end of the year the banks, the City and the government had become involved. By the middle of 1973 a solution appeared to have been found, but in September the workforce was told that Meriden was to be closed. Their reaction was predictable and their

Same 1971 T100R in home-market form with megaphone silencers and different tank finish.

The T100R Daytona for 1973, really its last year, for few were built in 1974.

mood one of bitter anger that their successful firm, with its tight-knit management team, had been so treated.

Thus began the Meriden sit-in, which was to last some 18 months until March 1975. During this time, there was a change of government, which resulted in left-winger Tony Benn being allowed to set up a workers co-operative at Triumph. This was to run on but, despite the loyalty of the workforce, was never a real success.

The trauma at the factory had less effect on the Tiger 100 than might have been expected. The two models were built for 1971 and 1972, became one for 1973 and even reached the 1974 range. However, their production ceased in September 1973, so that of the last year was limited in output and the

machines were little altered from the previous year. The one change was to the silencers, which took a megaphone shape with a rounded reverse-cone end. The finish was in Ice white and Argosy blue in the 1973 style.

There was to have been one further development of the Tiger 100 as a Series 2 model, or T100D Daytona. This took the machine a step forward by incorporating a number of group components, while keeping much of that which existed. The most noticeable change was to a 10 in. disc front brake with the caliper mounted to the rear of the left-hand fork leg. The brake was hydraulically operated, and the whole system came from the larger 744 cc twins.

The same source provided the front forks, which had alloy sliders,

The TR5T Trophy Trail, or Adventurer, which replaced the T100C for 1973, but failed to survive the Meriden sit-in.

internal springs, hydraulic damping and gaiters to keep the weather at bay. The fork legs were polished, and each wheel spindle cap was held to the leg on four studs. At the rear went the group's conical hub in light-alloy with the rear sprocket bolted to it. The brake remained a 7 in.

Roy Peplow taking his Triumph twin to the 500 cc class win in the 1964 Vic Brittain trial.

Nasty weather for Roy Peplow during the speed test of the 1965 ISDT, held in the Isle of Man. Roy, a member of the Great Britain Trophy team, won a gold medal.

single-leading-shoe type with a torque arm to anchor the backplate, and the wheel was not at all quickly-detachable.

The remainder of the machine was much as before, but the silencers were as later used by the larger twins and of megaphone shape with a reverse-cone of shallow taper. The finish was in the standard blue and white, but only ten of these machines were built as a pilot batch.

After the long sit-in ended, the firm concentrated on the larger twins, so no more Tiger 100 machines were built. Thus ended the model name that had first been used in 1939, had seen a major revision for 1960, and had acquired a firm place in the hearts of all Triumph enthusiasts for all time.

# Competition

Although often overshadowed by the larger Bonneville twins and Trident triples, in time, the unit Tiger 100 assumed the mantle of its pre-unit predecessor. The first T100A may have had a distinctly touring image, but the arrival of the T100SS changed that, and the model went on to considerable successes, both on and off the road.

Trials work was not to be the unit twins forte, although the works team did use them for a while. The engine tended to be too sharp for the delicate art of finding grip where none existed, whether on greasy rocks or deep down in the mud. This characteristic was to make them better for ISDT work, a field in which Triumph had long had success.

This went back to the earliest days of the event, and in the postwar years their 1948 machine was developed into the TR5 Trophy model. During the 1950s the factory was involved in the ISDT for most years, both with a manufacturer's team and with a Triumph in the British Trophy or Vase teams.

In the 1960s, the ISDT Triumphs

Ken Heanes during selection tests in 1968; here he has to remove and replace the rear wheel against the clock.

John Giles on the twin has his card signed while S.Ducker awaits the signal to go on his Triumph Cub. The event is the Nomads Trial of 1970.

were usually of 649 cc capacity, and one of their best riders was Ken Heanes. He rode as a member of the British Trophy team many times and, when the manufacturers no longer supported the event, prepared his own machines. In 1967 this was a Triumph twin of 504 cc; for 1969 he ran a team of Triumphs.

For 1970 Heanes organised an ISDT team using Cheney Triumphs, which had the twin engine fitted to

Rickman Metisse having a small Triumph unit twin fitted in the nickel-plated frame - typical of the type.

cycle parts produced by Eric Cheney. Cheney was a very experienced and first-class scrambles rider who went on to build machines using his own design of frame. These were powered by a variety of engines, including Triumphs, and were beautifully constructed and very successful.

All of Cheney's machines reflected his meticulous approach and high-quality workmanship, so it was an easy choice for Heanes to make. The British team suffered problems in the early 1970s events, but did take second place for the 1973 Trophy.

The Rickman brothers worked to the same high standards as Cheney and had a similar successful scrambles background. From this came their Metisse scrambler, which

was powered by a pre-unit engine, and, in time, a whole series of immaculate frame kits. Among these was one for the T100 unit twin and similar engines, this kit offering the same excellent construction as all the others.

The Rickman Metisse was most successful, both commercially and in competition, but the twins that the factory scrambled suffered from having to be seen to be heavily based on the standard models. At first, the unit engines were found to lack stamina and have reliability problems, but lessons learned on the road racing circuits soon showed the way to the necessary answers.

For a brief while, one rider had his works Triumph engine installed in a BSA scrambles frame, which resulted in a fast machine that

At Bordon army camp in 1971, some work in hand on the Cheney Triumphs.

Gary Nixon at one of the events he competed in during 1967, the first year he won the Number 1 plate in the USA.

handled well. However, higher management decreed otherwise, despite the two firms being of one group, and the exercise was brought to a rapid halt. This attitude was never to change, and it held back the real potential of the twin until the team was disbanded.

The Triumph small unit twin was used for other specials besides those mentioned above. The engine would fit neatly into the Greeves frame

Nixon on his Triumph twin during his winning ride at the 1967 Daytona 200. Note the massive front brake.

with its cast-aluminium down-beam, so a number of such machines were built over the years for both road and trail use. Others were constructed using a variety of frames, the build standards reflecting each owner's skills in mating the parts together.

On the road racing circuits, the Tiger 100 was in action as early as 1962 when Don Burnett won the 200-mile Daytona race by the narrowest of margins. This prompted the factory to enter four works machines for the 1966 event, for which they were considerably reworked, both internally and externally. The team suffered many problems in the build-up to the race, but in the end, Buddy Elmore brought the factory machine home first, while another Triumph was second.

From this win came the model name 'Daytona' and the determination to try again in 1967. For that year, there were six machines, further developed, and they had very little trouble in practice. Often, such good fortune precedes a bad race performance, but not that year, for once again, the Triumphs were first and second, Gary Nixon being the winner.

Nixon won the Number 1 plate

To the winner, the spoils; Nixon after the 1967 Daytona 200 race with second-placed Buddy Elmore to his left. At the back, behind Nixon, stands Doug Hele from Triumph.

The 1968 works 500 cc Triumph, as raced by Percy Tait and similar to the Daytona machines.

that year and retained it by a slim margin in 1968, the year Ray Knight won the 500 cc class of the Production TT on his Triumph, and a Tiger 100 took the 500-mile production race. The factory began to run a racing 500 in selected home events to assist their development work, employing works tester Percy Tait as the rider. During 1969 he contested some rather more important events, his best result being a second to the MV Agusta of Agostini in the Belgian GP.

From then on, the factory concentrated its efforts on the triple, while the Bonneville continued as a dominant force in production machine events . It was, as always, ably supported in the 500 cc class by the Tiger 100.

Lew Ellis, competition manager of Shell, talking to Roy Peplow at the 1972 ISDT. Lew's experience went back to prewar Brooklands days, and he was a close friend of countless riders and drivers.

# Triumph T90/T100 Specifications

All models have a twin-cylinder, overhead-valve engine built in unit with a four-speed gearbox, telescopic front forks, pivoted-fork rear suspension, an alternator and one or two Amal carburettors.

| Model | T100A | T100SS | T100SC | T100SR | T90 | T100 |
|---|---|---|---|---|---|---|
| years | 1960-61 | 1962-65 | 1962-65 | 1963-65 | 1963-69 | 1966 |
| bore (mm) | 69 | 69 | 69 | 69 | 58.25 | 69 |
| stroke (mm) | 65.5 | 65.5 | 65.5 | 65.5 | 65.5 | 65.5 |
| capacity (cc) | 490 | 490 | 490 | 490 | 349 | 490 |
| comp ratio | 9.0 | 9.0 | 9.0 | 9.0 | 9.0[1] | 9.0 |
| carb type | 375[2] | 376 | 376 | 376 | 376[3] | 376 |
| carb size | 7/8[4] | 1 | 1 | 1 | 15/16[5] | 1 |
| ignition | ET[6] | coil | ET | coil | coil | coil |
| alternator | RM15 | RM19 | RM19 | RM19 | RM19 | RM19 |
| voltage | 6 | 6 | - | 6 | 6[7] | 12 |
| top gear | 4.80[8] | 5.33[9] | 5.64 | 5.70 | 6.04 | 5.70 |
| petrol - (gall) | 3.5 | 3.5[10] | 2.6[11] | 3[12] | 3[13] | 3 |
| front tyre | 3.25x17 | 3.25x19[14] | 3.25x19[15] | 3.25x19 | 3.25x18 | 3.25x18 |
| rear tyre | 3.50x17 | 3.50x18 | 4.00x18 | 3.50x18[16] | 3.50x18 | 3.50x18 |
| front brake dia | 7 | 7 | 7 | 7 | 7 | 7 |
| rear brake dia | 7 | 7 | 7 | 7 | 7 | 7 |

[1] - 1967-9.5
[2] - 1961-376
[3] - 1968-624
[4] - 1961-1
[5] - 1968-24 mm
[6] - in 1961 - coil
[7] - 1966-12
[8] - 1961-5.05
[9] - 1963-5.70
[10] - 1963-3, 1965-3.5
[11] - 1963-2
[12] - 1965-3.5
[13] - 1965-3.5, 1966-3
[14] - 1963-3.25x18
[15] - 1964-3.50x19
[16] - 1964-4.00x18

# Triumph T90/T100 Specifications

| Model | T100R | T100R | T100C | T100S | T100T | T100D |
|---|---|---|---|---|---|---|
| years | 1966 | 1967-74 | 1966-72 | 1967-70 | 1967-70 | 1974 |
| bore (mm) | 69 | 69 | 69 | 69 | 69 | 69 |
| stroke (mm) | 65.5 | 65.5 | 65.5 | 65.5 | 65.5 | 65.5 |
| capacity (cc) | 490 | 490 | 490 | 490 | 490 | 490 |
| comp ratio | 9.0 | 9.75[1] | 9.0 | 9.0 | 9.75[1] | 9.0 |
| carb type | 376 | 376(2)[2] | 376[2] | 376[2] | 376(2)[2] | 626(2) |
| carb size | 1 | 1-1/16[3] | 1[3] | 1[3] | 1-1/16[3] | 26 mm |
| ignition | coil | ET[4] | coil | coil | coil | coil |
| alternator | RM19 | RM19[5] | RM19[5] | RM19[5] | RM19[5] | RM21 |
| voltage | 12 | 12 | - | 12 | 12 | 12 |
| top gear | 5.40 | 5.40[6] | 5.70 | 5.70 | 5.70 | 5.70 |
| petrol - (gall) | 2 | 2[7] | 2[7] | 3 | 3 | 2 |
| front tyre | 3.25x19 | 3.25x19 | 3.25x19[8] | 3.25x18 | 3.25x18[9] | 3.25x19 |
| rear tyre | 4.00x18 | 4.00x18 | 4.00x18 | 3.50x18 | 3.50x18 | 4.00x18 |
| front brake dia | 7 | 7[10] | 7 | 7 | 7[10] | 10 disc |
| rear brake dia | 7 | 7 | 7 | 7 | 7 | 7 |

[1] - 1968-9.0
[2] - 1968-626
[3] - 1968-26 mm
[4] - 1968-capacitor
[5] - 1969-RM21
[6] - 1968-5.70
[7] - 1971-UK 3
[8] - 1967-3.50x19, 1971-UK 3.25x19
[9] - 1969-3.25x19
[10] - 1968-8